Echoes of a Broken Soul

Shannon Dickinson

Presentation by *BookLeaf Publishing*

Web: www.bookleafpub.com

E-mail: info@bookleafpub.com

ISBN: 9789363300316

First edition 2024

To my Tan Man -

Without you, these words wouldn't exist...

Te amo por la eternidad.

ACKNOWLEDGEMENT

Always having hope thanks to Emily Dickinson
and Nothing More...

PREFACE

These poems reflect a profoundly personal and emotional aspect of my life. They arise from my intense feelings about a situation that was deeply evocative and emotionally charged. These feelings are not a reflection of any one individual.

Caught in Her Spell

The way you taste,
The way you smell,
The way you feel,
Before you left me,
For Mary Jane.

You turn from me
And run straight to her
She doesn't love you
But you know no other name.

Fighting the raging in my head,
The closing throat,
The rolling stomach.

In her grip, so deep
You think of little else
But the way she feels
Though it's nothing
That actually soothes.

She manipulates you
You're someone new
It's not who I know,
It's something mean.

She won't give you up,
But I can't leave...

Don't worry,
I won't give you up,
It hurts knowing
I wasn't the one
You wanted to keep.

You turn from me
So quickly every chance
While I wait desperately
For your return
With open arms
And tears in my eyes.

You're stuck in her game
It kills me inside,
No matter, it's fine.
You stay away with her
Though she lingers so.

Her scent on your skin,
She haunts your eyes,
Forever on your breath,
Always in your lies.

I stayed when I shouldn't -
Waiting in the background,

Putting you first,
When she never would.

It's her you choose every time
Overall
Her hold on your life
But you, oblivious.

It's fine,
I've got this you say,
Though they are her words only.

Her lies become yours,
You no longer care,
Just to be in her embrace,
Whenever you can.

Even with me
She's always on your mind
When you get to see her again
Lose yourself under her spell.

Broken promises
Fill in the silence
It's never me you reach for,
You left me behind.

Waiting, hoping, wishing
That one day you'll return

To who you were
Before you left me,
For Mary Jane.

You forget me when you're with her
But love me more after
Your demons remain priority
While I, an abandoned thought.

I want you back
Not this person who lacks -
Get rid of the demons,
Then you'll stop fiending -
Of this habit break free,
Return to me -
You'll be peaceful again;
You have the power to win.

Considerate

5

I gave you my heart.

At least you refused
To look at me -

…when you shattered it…

All without flattery.

Eyes Never Lie...

I took your advice
And tried to smile,
But it never reached my eyes…

Silent Tears

7

Every night I cry myself to sleep.
The tears fall silent.
Reminding that I'll never be good enough.

Tú Cara

8

I no longer wished to be awake,
But stayed only to see your face.

Unconditionally Conditional

You managed to forgive those who -

Berate you
Degrade you
Negate you
Persuade you
Abuse you
Use you
Fool you
Left you.

Yet never forgave the one who -

Stood by you
Supported you
Comforted you
Encouraged you
Promoted you
Took care of you
Unconditionally loved you

…instead, you left.

Apologies in the Dark

Every night since you left me,
I've cried myself to sleep.

The tears, the only solace,
In knowing I'm still alive.

My heart, tired of grieving,
No longer wants to beat.

My head, knowing better,
Won't give up, just yet.

The fight is coming to a close,
All I can do is apologize, again.

The Silence Between Us

The tears falling, my only friends.
Your hollow words, won again.
It's me, I'm toxic.
But that doesn't stop it.
The happiness, I remember.
That stopped in December.
The promises, all broken.
Now everything left unspoken.
Of you, I was terribly fond.
My 11:11 to wish upon.
Something stopped, so abrupt.
So suddenly, my heart was crushed.
I miss the feeling, the touch constant.
Now you've become a stranger, distant.

Silent Temptations

The screaming in my heart is getting heavy
The silence becoming too loud
The pieces become jagged
As they fall apart

It's in the silence that the feelings come back
Unwanted, unwelcome, never forget
Just trying to survive the night
The quiet my only companion

The darkness soothing, a new lover
Convincing with its velvet tongue
Come over, it's fine, it's peaceful
The offer no longer off the table

No more silent screams alone in the night
Feeling every mistake on replay
Taking a breath and deciding
Is this one the last?

The Pain I Embrace

13

I wish I went numb when you left.
Instead I decided to feel more.
More of my heart breaking with every tear I
hide.
More of my stomach clenching with anxiety.
More of my head pounding with what ifs.
More of my lungs hiding the screams.
More of my whole being in agony.

The Cost of Hope

When I look at you,
I see what could have been,
But what will never be.
You can't forgive me for making human
mistakes
Trying to be better.
So, I need to accept it and move on.

I'm tired of crying.
I'm tired of feeling less than.
I'm tired of hoping.
I'm tired of hanging on to the what ifs when it's
clear they will never be.
I'm tired of feeling lonely.
I'm tired of being in agony.
I'm tired of feeling my heart break again with
each new day.
I'm tired of the scenarios in my head lying to
me.
I'm tired of you making me feel crazy.
I'm tired of hiding my heart from someone who
can't handle it.
I'm tired of your actions having no
responsibility.

I'm tired of the happy memories reminding me
why I cry.

15

I'm just tired…

A Heart Left Behind

We were unofficial –
I was loyal, you were not.

The feelings were unsure, but mutual –
I waited, you did not.

You pushed me away –
I remained, you did not.

The depth of betrayal –
You lied, I did not.

The amount of hurt created –
I still cared, you did not.

A tortured heart left –
You moved on, I did not.

Calendar of Pain

You made me hate Thanksgiving because I was
now just a side dish.
You made me hate Christmas because of your
false kisses.
You made me hate New Year's because my
resolution was you.
You made me hate my birthday because I wasn't
even worth a card.
You made me hate Valentine's because I didn't
deserve glitter.
You made me hate St. Patrick's because I got no
kiss as an Irish lass.
You made me hate Easter because your eggs
were at another house.
You made me hate the dark because the thoughts
consumed.
You made me hate the light because the tears
would show.
You made me hate Wednesdays because that's
the day you broke me.
You made me hate Fridays because it was silent
for the next sixty-four and a half.
You made me hate Sundays because I waited for
the door to never open.

You made me hate Mondays because I had to get out of bed and pretend.
You made me hate sleeping because you were always in my head.
You made me hate being awake because you were in every single thought.
You made me hate April Fools' because I was a fucking joke.

Paradoxical Peace

19

If I'm so happy, why do I still cry?
Why do I feel anger deep inside?
Could it be the nostalgia of who we were?
Could it be that we will never be the same?
Could it be that time is still healing?
Could it be the disbelief that you're proud I'm
yours?
Could it be the constant fear that you'll leave
again?

The Stranger Within

Someone was there looking in
Standing, creeping
But it was just me, hoping
Searching for that feeling long ago
Wishing for the moments
Wanting for the rush
Dreading the silent screams.

Knowing I let it go
Like dreams fading
I stood there, a stranger
Outside a realm of reality
Watching, waiting
For chances forever gone
Where did I go?

The Burn of Hope

Hope is the thing
That lingers in your soul.
It's also the thing with talons
That kills you nice and slow.
It gives you something to believe in
When everything seems grim.
Holding on to hope
Is a different kind of pain.
It allows the destruction
Of possibility to remain.
It can be unrealistic and full of disillusionment,
The existential crisis you suffer.
But faith and resilience proffered
To guide while lonely in the dark.
To rise from the ashes of all that had to burn
In the midst of struggle and strife.
Hope provides new life,
To choose between despair, yours alone, to
discern.

Love's Second Chance

A year and 3 months, I only wanted you.
But you wanted something easy and new.

You came back for the holidays, I was happy
again.
While simultaneously still with a "friend".

You left once more, then came the lies.
I didn't want to believe it, right in front of my
eyes.

We weren't even cold, it only took hours.
Making plans with another, that weren't ours.

You broke everything in me, left me on the floor.
All to be with your brand-new whore.

You pretended to be my friend but were a cruel
stranger.
The next 3 months of hell were a game changer.

You made mistakes and came back with tears.
But was an apology enough to alleviate my
fears?

My heart said yes, my brain – slow down.
Could we start over with the brand-new dawn?

Words are primitive, actions prove change.
Can I ever forgive and overcome this rage?

You are my forever, us against the world.
The feelings repressed in my heart once again
unfurled.

It's you and me – Texas Toast and Tan Man.
A wifey with her hubby at her side – together,
making a stand.

#Clappalations 27:7

The best things come out of the fire
The pain and torment of pure desire
Wanting what we can't have, waiting
Just a taste, fleeting, elating
Wishing, dreaming for you to be mine
Little did I know it would come in time
A need I didn't know I wanted
Your absence left my heart haunted
You pretended to be mine, then left it cold
Anger, hurt, sorrow all filled the void of woe
A million tears and more slipped down my face
Countless thoughts and pleas on you I did waste
Despite being broken and fucked up
You came back with a single touch
A heart to be repaired by trust
Again we were together, but a real us
Our lives bound by heartbreak and survival
A relationship new, but was again revived
We both learned many new lessons
Always and forever, my 27:7

Eternal Thirst

Your smell at midnight.
Your taste after hours apart.
Your mouth whispering at 3 am.
Your laugh in the rain.
Your hands in the car.
Your eyes in the light.
Your arms open wide.
Your smile a million meanings.
Your intellect sometimes arrogant.
Your style on point.
Your heart a juxtaposition.
Your courage fierce.
Your passion between sheets.
Your desire burning in those eyes.
Your humor in aphorisms.
Your honesty though brutal.

It will never be enough…

I need your smell on my skin, covering me with
sin.
I need your taste to intoxicate me through the
night.
I need your mouth, greedy on my neck and
rough.

I need your laugh, my siren song, my better half.
I need your hands touching me while we drive.
I need your eyes, my green light in the dark.
I need your arms, promising the world in one
embrace.
I need your smile, both devious and kind.
I need your intellect to forever grow and
consume with no limit.
I need your style to mimic and inspire my own.
I need your heart to heal beside mine, despite
being broken.
I need your courage to never back down, while
we repair what's been done.
I need your passion sparking my fire at all hours.
I need your desire to make me come alive, of
which I will never grow tired.
I need your humor through brevity and wit, but
with universal truth.
I need your honesty even with tears, but always
revealing.

You claim I will grow tired of it,
Of this fear, I will acquit.
You've sung your song,
An addiction so strong.
You're my ride or die,
I want you for life, but need you to defy.

Wild Hearts

In early gray dawn, where dreams dance,
A rhythm with our shared silhouette.
Our bodies speak only whispers and moans,
A symphony of secrets only we know.

Your touch sets fire, demanding, so bold,
In every curve and crevice, our story behold.
The way you linger, tracing every line,
Teeth on skin, driving me wild.

We weave a thousand threads,
In dreams and daylight, where thoughts soon
spread.
We play in realms provocatively entwined,
A meeting of hearts, a merging of minds.

Your laughter, a spark in our darkened place,
Eyes unwavering, face to face.
Through every jest and glance held,
In our slick dance, we revel.

A puzzle, a chess board ready,
Understanding each look, every subtle gaze.
A dialogue sans words, our silent play,
Feeding desires in clandestine ways.

We explore a world only ours,
In touches and moments that last hours.
Each kiss, a promise of what's to come,
Slowly, quickly, we become one.

In our tangled breath, touch, and thought,
A dance of passion that can't be forgot.
We explore the pleasure of our fate entwined,
In every caress and intimate design.

Your love the sword, broad and deep,
I became yours, for eternity to keep.
Both wise and wild in love,
We find our truth with nothing to prove.

Twin Flame

The other half of my soul mirrored
Yin to my yang, night to my day
London to my Fog, light in my heart
Patience to impatience, subduing the dark
Independence, bound by love.

A connection powered by challenge
Profound mourning, intense regret
Exhilarating allure, your song the cure
Empath, witchcraft, hypnotic fascination
Magnetic bond, emotions correspond.

Awake, discovering self, unending growth
Butterflies, dragonflies, releasing the beast
White moths, angel numbers increase
Pushing comforts boundaries
Fears and desires, quite the quandary.

Necessity of phase, moon with the sun
Situationship – intermission – relationship
Going from strong to unbreakable bond
One had to be lost to realize the cost
First the soul was broken, then built up

Metamorphic connection, our mission

Freedom to adventure, our hearts conquer
Travel anywhere in time, fingers entwined
Laughter, happiness, living in peace
A concept complex; a twin flame vortex.